VISCERAL OUTCRIES of a SOCIAL MORON

A book of poetry and commentary

by

Copyright © August 2, 2012 by Daniel W. Strasel
All rights reserved.
All text, photographs, artwork, and format by Daniel W. Strasel
Library of Congress Registration # TX 7-589-295

No part of this book may be used or reproduced in any manner whatsoever without written permission from the author.

Published by Daniel Strasel

 HTTP://www.Mirroranium.com

ISBN-13: 978-0-9859964-5-1

This page is blank.

(This page is a liar)

TABLE OF CONTENTS

FOREWARD	7
IAMBIC PENTAMETER	8
GAS STATION ROSE	9
THAT WHICH CALLETH	10
SILENCE	11
DESPERATION	12
DISPASSIONATE	13
A SIMPLE QUESTION	14
NOW	15
COFFEE	16
REMEMBER	17-18
SMOKING	19
RAMBLINGS	20
DRUNK DEAD GUY ON MY LAWN	21-22
LIFE ITSELF	23
SHATTERED	24
SHEEP	25
STOLEN ART	26
HERMIT	27
METAMORPHOSIS	28
AN OLD BENT MAN	29
REQUIEM	30
ATTRACTED TO DARKNESS	31
THE PUSSING YELLOW EYE	32-33
HEAT	34
VIOLENT KNIGHT	35-36
CHOOSE YOUR OWN ADVENTURE	37
IN YOUR ARMS	38
ONE DAY	39
DEMON	40
WRITERS	41
THE GORN	42

- [Daniel Strasel] -

TABLE OF CONTENTS

43	TERROR HOUR
44	ANSWER
45	ONLY ETERNITY
46	ZABETH
47	TIME
48	SIN
49	HERALD
50	ARTIFICIAL FLAVORING
51	EYE CONTACT
52	MISSION STATEMENT
53	UPON REQUEST
54	DREARY & MISSY MUZZ
55	BACKWARD
56	DRAW A REINDEER!
57	PERHAPS
58	ICED TEASPOONS
59	TO READER
60	ADDENDUM
61-62	VOX VERITAS
63	DUURACHEN
64	OF ANTHONY ANGER
65	FOR DANNA ON HER BIRTHDAY
66	NEVAR MORE
67-68	DOWN WITH THE QUEEN
69	CRYSTAL WOMEN
70	HAPPY AUTONOMY
71	MAINFRAME MONSTERS
72	JUST PIGGIN' AROUND
73-74	ONE FOOL MAKES MANY
75	WICHENED
76	THE END
78	ABOUT THE AUTHOR

- [Visceral Outcries of a Social Moron] -

FOREWARD

So I told my cousin that I was going to write a book.

"Really?" he said. "What kind of book?"

"Poetry, commentary, and possibly some illustration - certainly an eccentric piece," I replied.

"Well," he said, his tone betraying his disdain, "you're certainly not going to make any money with *that*."

IAMBIC PENTAMETER

Iambic pentameter - it simply won't do.

Untainted,
        Unchained,
                Are my words to you.

GAS STATION ROSE

Who could ever shy away
From a feeling felt so true
As inspired as to say
A little plastic "love you?"
Sentiments so deeply felt,
Proclaimed for all to see
That any simple frown must melt
And conjure smiles to be.
Real flowers wither and die
Nagging thoughts of end,
But gas station roses can defy
The hands of time and mend

                A broken heart.

So, let the earthly gardens fail!
Let them cease to grow!
For plastic roses stand up in hail
And bloom throughout the snow.

THAT WHICH CALLETH

That which calleth
From low our dreams
Cradles fear
And sings our screams

SILENCE

Silence
    Rolling through the grove
Fog
    Dripping down the tree trunks
    Blanketing the grass
A deep azure
    Cooling the fiery intent of life
    Flowing out into the world
    From a single still pool
    Fenced by white marble
    Guarded by granite angels
    Whose faces never smile
    Tho lightly crowned with faery dew
    And shining slightly
    With the elusive sun
    No spirit moves their heavy wings
    No life ignites their eyes
    And only pouring from their lips
Silence

DESPERATION

Into the bathroom
Bent over the toilet
Heaving and hurling
And thrashing about

Puking and puking
Some brown stuff
And corn

Corn, corn, CORN

And when I look
Into the deep recess
I feel again
The urge to purge
For seen betwixt
The poop and vomit
A dead little guy
On his white boat

I killed I killed
The Tidy Bowl Man
Help me God
The Tidy Bowl Man

DISPASSIONATE

Looking deep into the sky

Motionless

Staring into the stars
My eyes bleeding
With tears
I cannot stop

I inhale the world
I have become

Suddenly infinite

Cold
Wind blasting my face
Oh my God
Let my life go on forever
As it is
Or let it all end now

So I scream
With the voice
Of every man
Who has lost his soul

A SIMPLE QUESTION

When I began
To entertain your fancy
I was confident and secure
In your seduction

And now

I am as unsure
                As a child
With a heart pounding
To an overwhelming beat

And though these feelings
Are as warm as the sun
They are perhaps rivaled
Only by the dreadful realization
That we stand forever
On the stairs of goodbye

Can it be worth this distress?

Definitely.

NOW

Dare to feel
Experience expression
Speak vividly
And become extreme
Disrobe thy caution
Silence concern
Denounce fear
Absorb life
Rise and conquer
Create unbound
Illuminate us
With thy soul
Unleash the lightning
Divide society
Construct Jehovah
With thy dreams

As ending night
Or shining start
Only ever art thou
Who ye think thou art

COFFEE

Coffee
Is the thought
That keeps me sane
It is the sweet
Elixir of life
The ultimate temptation of man

And so
Do I give my soul
For Coffee
Sweet Coffee
Great Coffee
I love you
Amen

REMEMBER

Oh, how I dread the setting of the sun

                        When night must come to quell the land

Oh, how I mourn the passing of the plate

                        For nothing else seems so gratifying

Oh, how I hate when the symphony fails

                        And the music comes to a halt

Oh, how I hesitate at the last page

                        For the story has been so good

    Though the movie has ended and the credits rolled
    I alone sit in the theater
    Though the heat from the water is fading fast
    I alone stand in the shower

    How I will miss the caress of your hand
    Or mysterious look in your eyes!
    How I will miss being close to you
    Your mind, soul, and body!
    How I will treasure all of our time
    Spent and yet to be!

How I will:

See your face mistakenly all the time on strangers

Feel a phantom of heat when I think of you

Secretly weep unaccountably at times

Stumble when I see you

Be silent when I try to talk to you

Walk loudly to cover the beating of my heart

Want to call you all the time

Call you and hang up before I dial the last number

Write numerous letters that I will never deliver

Type this in agony

Rub my eyes, everyone thinking I'm tired

Miss you

Drive past your house, just for proximity

Not be able to get my work done

See you and smile

Wonder

Look forward to when I can meet with you

Remember

SMOKING

Smoking is the universal sign
Of peace on Earth, goodwill towards man

It's not that **we** don't know -
It's that **they** don't know
Them
Those people
The collective group of humankind
Who do not smoke

They'll never know a taste
Of the instant friendship
Between smokers on break together

And when I think on this
I discover
They don't *deserve* to smoke
Stupid
 Socially malnourished
  Hypocritical
   Uppity
    Demented
     Bastards
May you burn, yet never smoke

- [Daniel Strasel] -

RAMBLINGS

I cannot begin to

Try

To understand
The conversational ambience
In this society

Yet

Perhaps that is only
The desperate measure
That we invariably gravitate towards
In order to justify our deviancy

Or perhaps
That is just me
Attempting to ratify
My dissention

DRUNK DEAD GUY ON MY LAWN

Flamingoes

And a beach ball on my lawn
But come no closer now
When the snow's too hot
Come no closer now
The winos are shot
Dead on my lawn

Burn you
Bind you
Death consign you

Drunk dead guy on my lawn

And my umbrella
Will open the gate
Hate
Hate
Don't touch my flamingo!
Don't play with my ball!
So soon will you be
A drunk dead guy on my lawn

Madmen

Playing dead party games
Burning dead bison
In a great black bonfire
Shining their rusty car keys
In your crusty face

- [Daniel Strasel] -

The skeleton's smiling

A bottle of Chardonnay
Brimming with evil

But come no closer now
Play no party games
Come no closer now
To where the drunk dead guys lay

Burn you
Bind you
Death consign you
Turn you
Tie you
Bondage blind you
Dunk you
Drunk you
Destruct your song

As you sing leeringly
A drunk dead guy on my lawn

LIFE ITSELF

Life itself
Is not a passive entity
But a ravenous beast
Whose hunger never quells
It devours anything
And kills everything
That cannot die

SHATTERED

The machinations of God
Annoy me
I want to shatter everything
Consume mankind
Violate nature
Desecrate creation
From Genesis to now
Burn
Rape
Maim

It's not hate

It's disgust

Loathing

Breathing in pain
At the mere thought
I shall ever have to look at you again

SHEEP

Sheep, sheep, lemonade
Hopefully, no sense is made
Carefully counting
Earnestly shouting
"Drop your clothes - begin the mounting!"

Sheep, sheep, for sale or trade
Just sell enough to make the grade
Never applying
Always defying
Nonsensical prose, yet still I'm denying

Sheep, sheep, that's what I said
Approaching the end, to black I fade
Noble intentions
At poetry conventions
Allow me to voice my sheepish intentions.

STOLEN ART

And now all the art is gone
Stolen by its maker
The table emptied by some girl
...Except the sugar shaker,
Salt and pepper, table tent,
Some stupid coffee tin;
Am I in a coffee house
Or am I in Berlin?
The music's old and out of date,
Everyone's clothes in tatters.
The restroom line is three miles long,
Awaiting anxious bladders.
I'll have to pee all over the floor
Or maybe on the table
-Maybe on the other guests-
Who said I was stable?

HERMIT

Alone, a shattered man does sit

No one near to witness it

No one here to see him cry

No one here to wave goodbye

METAMORPHOSIS

Roaming the hillside
Searching the air
Screaming, screaming, at the find
Running from the horrid sight
Covering chaste eyes
Tears of acid dropping to stain the ground
Nightmare horrors arise silently
Talking to the crowd
"**Lies become you**" they would say
To the people of the day
Fiends who walk the night
Smashing souls with their spirit hammers
Destroying that which grows between
Lost in bitter sorrow
Searching for the single truth
That found was never lost
Metamorphosis
Metal that never gleamed so bright
Perpetual losses found again
The mind cleared of
The waste and taint
The cold, cold, soil
The sun, striking the barren Earth
Washing it of plague
Shadows dissolve, and men stand
To forget another day

AN OLD BENT MAN

An old bent man
With cross in hand
Crossing lightly
The light of life
Gripping tightly
Hope unsightly
Hoping wholly
For holy help
Clouds parted
Understanding started
Startled under
Savior's brow
Reveling in redemption
And in revelation

Revealing love

REQUIEM

Once again the bloodthirsty scream
The bold defiance, my life, my dream
My horror profound
The hellfire sound
As the black violins lift their bows to the theme

Though barely seen
And kneeling silent
Cover my ears
Smile defiant
An oboe rises
Slowly falls
Piano pounds
To its calls
Order plummets
Chaos breaks
Foundation trembling
Reality shakes
Kettle booming
Voice of doom
Mouthing mayhem
To the room
Triumphant trumpets
Steal the sound
Within the melody
So am I drowned

A gurgling, a popping. I cannot go on
Hands on my ears o'er bloodstains long
Then slowly I turn
My eyes brightly burn
As I see the dark queen, her words with the song

THE PUSSING YELLOW EYE

If you look high
Into the sky
You will spy

The pussing yellow eye
(That one that sits nigh
Inside the sky)
'Twill make you cry:
"Oh my, Oh my!
"What is that... horrible... pussing eye?"

But don't rely
On passers by
To begin to comply
To your silly cry
...They'll either laugh or merry sigh

If you look high
Into the sky
You will spy

The pus, dripping to low from high
And landing quite noisily upon your thigh
And whether you walk or run awhy
- No matter how hard you try -
You'll never destroy that yellow dye
Either from on your thigh
Or on your tie
You'll be cursed forever by
This gigantic and monstrous sty

If you look high
Into the sky
You will spy

The pussing yellow eye
(That one that sits nigh
Inside the sky)
'Twill all reason starkly defy
By living forever, never to die
Or care that your thigh
Will never be dry

Although you now vie
For IN san ah TIE
There's a point to all this, I'll tell you why:

Although some like their pus on wheat or rye,
I *strongly* suggest it in pussing yellow pie.

ATTRACTED TO DARKNESS

So this is it
The culmination of life
So strange to look down
Upon the entirety of existence
To be repulsed
And seduced
Simultaneously

HEAT

Under the heat
I watched, I prayed
The crescendo resounded,
Yet on the band played
Over the waves
I spied a lass
Whose only intent
To wedge the mass
Yet not a tear
Sprung from my eye
Over the roar
I heard her cry
A heartfelt whisper,
Lost forever
Betwixt the shouts
O'er the crowd's endeavor
With sudden resolve
I nodded slow
And without seeing
I felt her woe
Now days have passed
Tho' ravens yet peck
At her wide staring eyes
And rope-strangled neck.

VIOLENT KNIGHT

Violent Knight
Unholy Knight
Nothing's calm
Nothing's bright
All lay dead
Beneath your sight
Torn from life
Unholy might
Seethe an evil peace
Seethe an evil peace

Dreadful Night
Endless Night
Burning ever
Flames of fright
Cities leveled
Lost their height
Motels vacant
No candlelight
Seethe an evil peace
Seethe an evil peace

Earthly site
Graveyard site
Far from beyond
Did come this wight
Who purges wrong
And purges right
Mindless function
Of sculpting blight
Seethe an evil peace
Seethe an evil peace

Violent Knight
Unholy Knight

All is gone
Goodly and trite
Heartlessly ending
The human plight
Should mankind survive
His nuclear bite
Seethe an evil peace
Seethe an evil peace

CHOOSE YOUR OWN ADVENTURE

Opening the book, you find yourself flipping through the pages almost carelessly. As you happen upon this page, something causes you to hesitate.

Having read the contents of the page, you quickly determine that you need to take action immediately.

You must choose:

A) I forgot to read *'Drunk Dead Guy on my Lawn!'*

(Turn to page #20)

B) I wonder what's next?

(Look at next page)

C) I am hungry and bored.

(Eat book)

**E-Book note: As you cannot 'eat book,' instead think of it as saying 'eat computer,' or whatever medium you are using to read this.

IN YOUR ARMS

Count not the years upon my face
Nor aging in my stance
Though finally I have lost my grace
For sake of such I dance

Say not the words I wish to hear
Nor look upon my form
Just mouth a whisper in my ear
For that will keep me warm

Simply said, I am content
With all your little charms
Closely held, I smell your scent
Dreaming in your arms

ONE DAY

Upon a sightless face I sat
Thinking solemnly of outstretched aeons
Upon which I have not tread

DEMON

I know a demon
His name is mine
He taunts me with dreams
And teases with smiles
Delighted with my torture
He plots ever on
Trying to frame me
Within his vision

WRITERS

I pray you smile upon my work
For in my heart an endless murk
To you I send this simple plea:
Let my actions worthy be!
Unite the pen and paper past
Let this be within our grasp
For only writers are the teachers
Read aloud by schoolhouse preachers

THE GORN

Beside a fitful lake
Does a gaping mouth of stone
Turn and twist the rushing wind
Into everlasting moan

Anon the night in its desire
Will call the dreadful Gorn
Let mothers lock their doors at night
And to their children warn

Staggeringly unerringly
While holding high its head
And to the light it cannot reach
It wails a rhyme of dread

Beyond the sight of Earthly eye
Lay charging, slow in measure
A beast, infernal, grinning slight
Such smiles of toothy pleasure

There is a horror greater
Than even soulless men can whim
As Fredrick, who is now the Gorn
Knows it to be him

TERROR HOUR

And then the sun died
In a crimson-orange oblivion
So night raped the world
Let swift death
Fall upon us
Let our dreams
Flow sweetly into
Terror
Nightmare
So shall the daughters
Stab the fathers
Destroy the oceans
Drink the waters
Poison life
Everlasting
Never lasting
Evermore

ANSWER

Will I ever find peace?
-Only in short respites-
As I forget who I am
And ignore who I was
To someday mistakenly
Blunder back into awareness
That any madness of normalcy
I might entertain
Is as a phantom

I mustn't rest,
Yet cannot go on
Believing in gods
That are benevolent

ONLY ETERNITY

Only eternity has passed
Since the soft sound of your voice
Sang me to delightful repose
Allow me a moment
To eviscerate my heart
And lay it out for all to see
A tender course unguarded

Only eternity has passed
Since the sweet delicacy of your beauty
Stunned me into utter silence
Let my eyes crawl longingly
Up and down your visage
Desiring with visceral hunger
A morsel so textured with fear

Only eternity has passed
Since the joy of your companionship
Drove me to an enlightened insanity
Weaving prose in remembrance of thee
Must I wait eternally more
Anticipating eagerly
Thy voice, thy beauty, thy touch?

ZABETH

Curious and worldly
Loved, yet silent
Searching, screaming
For untainted solace
Unsure, yet condemning
Wounded, yet strong
Defiance
Need

A void where there should be none

Someday, someone
Something will come
To destroy
This unforgiving illusion
Seen only by she

TIME

Time is ravaging me
Tearing me apart
Holding me down
Every morning I wonder

-Is it me?-

Another tick of the clock
Another moment gone
Another memory lost
Only to be replaced

With this one

Oh no
Not this one

No

No

No, don't let it be this...

This thief of meaning
This irrelevant conjunction
Between before and soon

SIN

Do not forgive me
For I have sinned
Not against you, Lord
But against myself
A crime for which
There can be
No redemption

HERALD

At the sound
Of a thousand crying
And at the light
Of a thousand flames
And at the instant
Of a thousand dying
And at the utterance
Of a thousand names

Will I come to conquer you

Will I bring D'Zannin to

Will I deathly deal do

Will I fate's decree issue

ARTIFICIAL FLAVORING

(Or "Sorta Peach")

On occasion, I have enjoyed eating foods or candy that have been made justifiable with artificial flavoring.

However, I would ultimately appreciate some sort of disclaimer on the packaging if it's not actually **succeeding** at tasting as it is allegedly supposed to.

Let's take, for instance, the peach pie I am eating right now. It's *close* to peach, but it's not dead on. Maybe the product could be relabeled as: "Our version of Peach," rather than calling it simply peach...because it's *not* peach, it's just *sorta* like peach.

EYE CONTACT

Eye contact
Is over rated
Almost worthless
As I stated
And yet now
I feel struck dumb
Under your gaze
Totally numb

Flailing
Helpless
Hopeless
Unarmed
Wooed
Attracted
Smitten
Charmed
Freedom, beauty, truth, love
Bohemian ideals spoken of
Cannot repair
And cannot raze
Further my heart
Beneath your gaze
I'm unaccustomed
To this hex
Struck down with love
And not with sex

And it may be all
And it may only be
And yet, still enough
Still enough for me

MISSION STATEMENT

Let me be accepting of other's shortcomings
Let my soul be filled with
love
Let my productions be filled with
worth
Let my truths all be
self-evident
Let me require excellence
in all that I do
Let me not worry about
money
Let me be content
with what I have
Let me always do the right thing

But

If I need to do the wrong thing
Let it affect everyone globally,
Or no one at all

UPON REQUEST

Raven black hair
Reflecting the neon
Of the nightlife
And the wightlife
Of Hamilton ere
When she's dancing
And prancing
And showing the world
How she's free from constraints
Of a boy or a girl
To the awe and wonder
Of a perilous crowd
There lay over granite
A mourner's shroud
So desperate to live
Yet dying inside
Declaring that love
Is as sinful as pride
...And yet the crime
Against the human race
Is seeing but joy
On that angel face

I am no devil
And yet no saint
What passes here now
Let me make quaint
If there be one thing
That makes it worthwhile
It is the honor of being
Present when you smile

DREARY & MISSY MUZZ

Dreary is as Dreary does
Mutely muttered Missy Muzz
Pointing her finger
And slapping her stick,
Not like an asshole
More like a
        Lady.

So Dreary did as Dreary would
And Missy rid herself of 'could'
Biting her pencil
And jumping the fence
Not like the ladies,
More like the
        Horses.

Dreary came and Dreary went
And Missy, finally, was spent
Writing her thoughts
Whilst whistling along
Not like a poem
More like a
        Story.

BACKWARD

Then again, I thought in reflection to the conversation with my cousin, *if I don't make money with **this**, then how am I to make it?*

Broccolodeon

After inserting a sprig of broccoli into the chassis of the Broccolodeon, one will be rewarded with music.

This is a million dollar idea.

DRAW A REINDEER!

E-book note: If you cannot draw in your current medium, go and fetch a piece of paper and an instrument with which you might draw and commence translating your thoughts into art.
You should only allow yourself one try.

PERHAPS

Perhaps it is, I am an image:
Easily shattered
Easily shamed
Tho with this work you glimpse my visage
Forever untattered
Forever unchanged

ICED TEASPOONS

　　I firmly believe that the Iced teaspoon is not given it's necessary credit.
　　Curiously slender and built to allow for more bites from less food, I consider it the most elegant of the spoon family. In addition, the Iced teaspoon surely sets the standard for the rest of the genus as no other spoon will share it's particular dimensions.
　　Coffee spoons and soup spoons have more considerable character, but lack that certain majesty that the Iced Teaspoon radiates. Baby spoons may attempt to out-classify the Iced Teaspoon, however the Baby spoon could only accommodate the most inexperienced of stomachs, and therefore is left wanting when examined more closely. The gargantuan ladle is so estranged from the Iced teaspoon, one can barely perceive the relationship.
　　In summary, please consider the Iced teaspoon when next you vote for your spoon of choice.

TO READER

This is my art. It is my gift to you, and to all mankind. It is what I feel compelled to do, and I do not exercise my attention to it lightly.

So thank you...

However, should you happen to be in possession of this book because you purchased it and you don't like it - I'm sorry.

I would love to offer you a money-back guarantee...but I cannot afford to buy it back.

Your dollar need not be unnecessarily spent, however! I hear it makes excellent kindling for the fireplace on cold nights. Or, if you carry it around with you, it doubles as a good luck talisman. Finally, this book is reputed to be an excellent source of emergency toilet paper.

E-book note: As those suggestions do not apply under these particular circumstances, I suppose your dollar was then, in fact, unnecessarily spent.

You should probably continue to purchase my literature until you find something you like.

ADDENDUM

    I am an imperfect person. I make transgressions against my brothers and sisters **constantly**, despite any regular exercises of compassion and empathy.
    I have been ungrateful, selfish, murderous, lustful, insatiable, proud, judgmental, sacrilegious, doubtful, unjust, unmerciful, unkind, deceitful, angry, vengeful, hateful, antisocial, unmutual*, violent, pitiful, righteous, fake, hypocritical, self-centered, manipulative, blasphemous, unfaithful; Worst of all, I have been completely aware of these transgressions *as they were happening.*

    I ask you to forgive me - in reflection of my iniquity, I am truly sorry and am trying very hard to be a better man than I have been.

*6

VOX VERITAS

The very concept of truth is significant *only* when measured between multiple perspectives. The value of the truth that is perceived from a single perspective need never be challenged.

Always keep an open mind when deliberating with another. In order to do this, you must have a segment of your understanding that is dedicated to the concept that *your* perspective of the subject is not necessarily the *correct* perspective. If you cannot entertain this idea, it is *pointless* to engage in such reflective dialogue.

Popular opinion so often replaces the truth with the convenience and comfort of acceptability.

Many of your understandings are simply a result of the teaching of the popular truth of your culture, and you must challenge yourself to unlearn some of that which you have been taught. I guarantee some of your accepted popular truths are in fact, flawed. A vicarious understanding is sometimes the most deplorable of all.

Invariably, most dialogues of contrasting perspectives devolve into disproving the opposing side rather than proving one's own. Breaking another person's dogma should not be the focus of your dissertation, however, so much as ratifying your own clever assumptions. After all, if the intent of debate is the establishment of truth: present your own understandings nobly, and listen as much as you speak.

When conversational discourse starts to degrade in the aforementioned manner, it becomes necessary for all individuals to establish and agree on self-evident and objective truths. Subjective truths are critical to the individual, but cannot hope to thrive long in the presence of another. Contrary-wise, subjective truths that are realized *as subjective* by the *subject* that holds to these truths become the most critically understood truths of that same *subject.*

Try not to get *too* involved in your own conclusions (as many of them were born of faith and not in fact), and always listen to another person's perspective: not being able to weigh a different perspective against your own will ultimately lead to your own destruction. Beware of your vindications!

- [Daniel Strasel] -

Emotion is a terrible and wonderful thing. Much like reflective thought can influence your reality, emotion can alter it. One must recognize and subdue (yet not eradicate) the emotional component of their psyche. Important that you do not make too many conclusions when you understand that your emotional engine has been primed and is running.

Having come to clarity, live upright. Be more than what you have been, if only for your own salvation. Now is the time.

DUURACHEN

Duurachen   Duurachen

Rise up and feed,
Oh mighty
        Oh terrible

Duurachen   Duurachen

Rise up, Rise up
Oh powerful
        Insatiable

Duurachen   Duurachen

Rise up and cry
Born again
        Die again

Duurachen   Duurachen

DUURACHEN!

- [Daniel Strasel] -

OF ANTHONY ANGER

Jobbleston Creek was always a ride
Quiet and spooky and wrinkled inside
Dull, almost gross, and riddled with fear
Quiet and hidden, yet curiously near

E'er did I step with reckless footfalls
'Twixt Anger's mansion's broken walls
Only to find what others may dread:
Hollow and timeless, old Anthony's head

FOR DANNA, ON HER BIRTHDAY

Dearest, darling, loving wife
   Who gives me all the best in life
     From smiling sweetly
     Or brandishing knife,
        Carefree caresses and endless strife:

I bid thee many a happy return!
   Though more for Seuss does thy heart burn
   Than for **this** choice, so I discern -
Hence that note, let us sojourn

To somewhere more whimsical,
   Wonderful,
   Impossibly bright,
With rainbow-filled days -
   No mention of night

   (Except at the end, when you turn out the light
      And whisper '*I love you*'s' to young ears' delight:
         The final remark in the ritual 'goodnight.'
            Sometimes so easy, yet sometimes a fight).

But I've gotten off track
   Derailed, I mean
     (But still, I enjoy the something between)
Now back to those rainbows!
   And green caviars
     And jelly-filled pickles
       And hiccupping stars…

Oh wait just a moment,
   What was it you want?
A thorough foot rub
   O'er literary jaunt?

I suppose I should end this
   And commence such duty
For my sweet, silly wife
   And her endless beauty.

- [Daniel Strasel] -

NEVAR MORE

"Excuse me now, though I must tarry -

Speaking plainly, unless very!

To wit...I put some sands upon the shore?"

What can I, right now be saying?

- Did I reason while dismaying -

Skittering and stammering as I never had before

Right through my legs, held fast to core.

"What had I had just been seeing?

Did it dungeon in the deeing?

Well, yes! We took those dwarves to Erebor!"

So...speaking clearly is no matter

By which I can offer flatter

(and thoughtless words are nothing better than a bore),

Thus I spake this "Nevar more."

DOWN WITH THE QUEEN

(From God, Man, and The Machine)

Faith over fact, you're always unseen
Your politics: boring, trite, obscene
Tired of trading life for a dream?
Water to wine? So where's my canteen?
I'm nursing a child who cannot wean
Milk without curd, yet all of the cream
I could become the *new* Magdalene
Basking in glory, looking quite preen
Move over Christ, make way for Christine
A better measure, *my* new regime
So dirty, your version. Mine, pristine
Stop talking about it! Let's begin:

The God, The Man, Misspoken Doctrine
Teaching you how to be a latrine
Don't settle for story, plot, or scheme!
Don't wait for the Deus Ex Machine!
NOW
Raise up your fists, yell Down with the Queen!
Down with the Queen!
Raise up your fists, yell Down with the Queen!

Chung might argue Monican or Breen;
Kubrick and Clark suggested something
Like Ellison's mouth which cannot scream
Like Gibson, punk, with none of the steam
Will without thought, created the lien
Dressings of blue, yellow, red, and green
Without the panes, yet always a screen
Backgrounds plenty, all part of the theme
Prick your finger and we'll splice the gene
No more *arousal, appendix, spleen...*
Presenting the way it *should* have been:
Without an end, yet always a mean

The God, The Man, Misspoken Doctrine
Teaching you how to be a latrine
Don't settle for story, plot, or scheme!
Don't wait for the Deus Ex Machine!
NOW
Raise up your fists, yell Down with the Queen!
Down with the Queen!
Raise up your fists, yell Down with the Queen!

CRYSTAL WOMEN

(From <u>God, Man, and The Machine</u>)

Burning Brightly through the night,
Tigress hunting, yearning height.
What immortal hand or eye
Will save this little cutie pie?

After hours, in the bowers
I reveal my magic powers:
Little crystal, with a whistle
Women flock to shoot this missile
Look for the whore, give her some more
Watch her resolve fall to the floor

I can use her and abuse her
And so long as I infuse her
She'll feel real; made of steel
Making love like pounding veal
Never sleeping, reason seeping
Planting only for my reaping

- *Instrumental bridge* -

Decay ruthless. Mouthing toothless
Sayings that are all but soothless
Fingers tearing without caring
At the facial flesh she's wearing
Now she's broken, can't be woken
Memory's her only token

Burning Brightly in her dreams
Tigress screaming without screams
What immortal hand or eye
Dare save this little Lorelei?

- [Daniel Strasel] -

HAPPY AUTONOMY

(From <u>The Terrors of Wonder</u>)

Assemble then, unto thee
At ONE (to *thou*, though <u>*Now*</u> *I* see)
Both Kings *and* Queen: the trilogy -
Yea, *all* the *silver* royalty -
That this fruit may given be
To the *darkest* of the three:
By visage, soul, or industry.

This choice be given unto *she*
- *Heiress* to the Company –
(Daddy's private novelty)

To the lock, I put the key
Your chains undone; you're finally free!
Free to be your very own *'Me!'*
Now thy*self*! Bereft of *He*
Eff, En, Oh, Are, Dee!
Birthday present *and* decree:
- *Happy New Autonomy*! -

MAINFRAME MONSTERS

(From The Terrors of Wonder)

They're there, they're *there* - they're there in the walls
The rooms and corr'dors, chambers and halls
Not there to assist you, nor right any wrong
Just waiting and hoping it won't take too long

Now if you are good, you might just agree
There's no need to fear for your family
But if you so slightly defy the hive
The mainframe monsters will eat you alive

Eat you alive! Make public your sin!
Eat you alive – but where to begin?
Tear you apart from present to past
One small misstep will soon be your last

We're there, *we're* there - we're there in the wings
Thinking up dang'rous 'n dreadful things
And that which we swore that we never would say
We said in our youth, and today's a new day

Now this understood, you now just might see
The mainframe monsters are you and me
Fearing each other, that we might contrive
To eat ourselves 'n each other alive

Eat you alive! Make public your shame!
Eat you alive – and isn't it plain?
We'll tear you apart mercilessly
All for a fleeting moment of glee

*

What black soul could conceive such a thought
That mankind could ever be easily bought?
Yet monsters we have, and we have become
When finding our faults is justice for fun

- [Daniel Strasel] -

JUST PIGGIN' AROUND

(From <u>The Terrors of Wonder</u>)

Once upon a time inside an old deserted barn
There lived a piggy family who loved their run-down farm
For such a place, although remote, was fun and fancy free
And many other animals soon joined the piggies three

Just piggin around.

Now outside in the wilderness, the wolves began to creep
They'd eat those pigs for breakfast, if not for several sheep
Who call themselves the guardians of this pig ridden town
Where most are busy piggin, or just piggin around

Just piggin around,
Just piggin around,
Just piggin aroun – ou –ou – ound
Just piggin around,
Just piggin around,
Just piggin aroun – ou – ou – ound

Just piggin around

ONE FOOL MAKES MANY

(From The Terrors of Wonder)

One fool makes many
All fools love money
So print off plenty
And let's get funny
We'll dance in the rivers
And swear up at the sky
Then we'll give unto the givers
And then lay at home and cry
One fool makes many
All fools love money
So give us plenty
Cause we're so funny
Now we'll sing unto each other
As we watch our lives roll by
Like our fathers and our mother
Sang our darkest lullaby
One fool makes many
All fools love money
Yet those with plenty
Don't act so funny
Money
Money
Money

The piper is there, the piper is calling
The money is false, the banks are falling
The lord awaits, so why are we stalling?
The truth is so true, the answer's appalling

- [Daniel Strasel] -

One fool makes many
All fools love money
So print off plenty
And let's get funny
We'll dance in the rivers
And swear up at the sky
Then we'll give unto the givers
And then lay at home and cry
We'll dance in the rivers
And swear up at the sky
Then we'll give unto the givers
And then lay at home

and cry

WICHENED

(From <u>The Terrors of Wonder</u>)

Wholly weary with 'which end?'
To wit: a wit with which, ends?
Then hearken, ye with wish, and
Receive the words of Wichened!
Waste the worry (which wits end),
Woes, and wants which with will send
The heart (with will which wilts) and
The head (with will which will stand)
To stand stone walls which withstand
The truth of which is which and
Wear only wounds - which, with sand
Will mend…at least with wit's end.

Put another broccoli in
In the Broccolodeon
  All I really wanna hear is
Music
  Music
    Music

THE END

OTHER ~~OUTCRIES~~ BOOKS

by Daniel Strasel

WITHOUT REST
ISBN 978-0-9859964-4-4

A tale of love and madness. When he confronts the Truth, a lovesick god has all of his dreams turned into nightmares.

THE TERRORS OF WONDER
ISBN 978-0-9859964-4-4

A tragicomedy about truth, identity, and leadership. A prominent young child with disturbing visions must overcome an intimate enemy or be lost forever.

GOD, MAN, AND THE MACHINE
ISBN 978-0-9859964-3-7

A story of symbols; a book of philosophy and fiction. An uninteresting man of mistaken importance struggles to understand his role in life.

Stegosaurus the Triceratops
ISBN 978-0-9859964-6-8

A book made to create great conversations: ethics of work, principle, helping, and leadership. A stuffed toy dinosaur encourages others by expressing care.

For Daniel's complete portfolio please visit Mirroranium.com

ABOUT THE AUTHOR

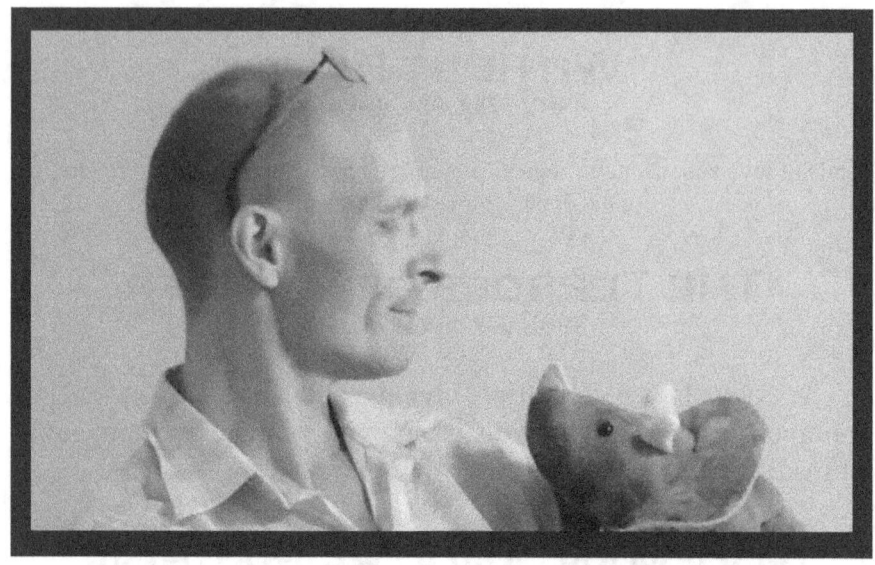

"I just wanted to make some art. I hope you like it."

Daniel Strasel, born September 15, 1973, sole progeny of ~~a blind tax collector~~ an eccentric, yet intelligent nurse named Sue. He emerged into life a genuine, happy child. Soon thereafter, he grew into a brooding and self-centered adolescent. A wild, ambitious, and impressionable young adult was followed by a confused, frightened, and purposeless man.

Following his tweens he finally found humility, discipline, and compassion before his overdeveloped sense of self-importance destroyed him completely.

Thanks always to my wife for helping provide the time for me to write this.